Whispers
of
Inspiration

Demetrios Trifiatis

inner child press, ltd.

Credits

Author

Demetrios Trifiatis, Ph.D.

Editor

hülya n. yılmaz, Ph.D.

Cover Design

William S. Peters Sr.
&
inner child press, ltd.

General Information

Whispers of Inspiration

Demetrios Trifiatis

1st Edition: 2019

This Publishing is protected under Copyright Law as a "Collection". All rights for all submissions are retained by the Individual Author and or Artist. No part of this Publishing may be Reproduced, Transferred in any manner without the prior *WRITTEN CONSENT* of the "Material Owner" or its Representative Inner Child Press. Any such violation infringes upon the Creative and Intellectual Property of the Owner pursuant to International and Federal Copyright Law. Any queries pertaining to this "Collection" should be addressed to Publisher of Record.

Publisher Information

1st Edition: Inner Child Press
intouch@innerchildpress.com
www.innerchildpress.com

This Collection is protected under U.S. and International Copyright Laws

Copyright © 2019: Demetrios Trifiatis

ISBN-13: 978-1-970020-80-9 (inner child press, ltd.)

$ 16.95

Dedicated to my beloved wife Anastasia,
my inexhaustible source of
love, serenity and understanding!

Table of Contents

Acknowledgements — xv
Preface — xvii
Foreword — xix
Introduction — xxi

A Poem Extraordinaire — xxiii
World Day Against Racism — xxvii

The Poetry

Life ... Man ... Destiny ... Nature ... Environment ... Cosmos — 5

Once Born	6
All I Am	6
Life's Sailing	6
Forgiving Life	6
The Rising Sun	7
The Dream	7
Walking Under the Sun	7
Swimming Upstream	8
An Eventful Life	8
Cosmic Dance	8
The Breath of Life	9
Once upon a Time . . .	10
Poetry	12
Flowers	12

Table of Contents ... *continued*

My Odyssey	13
One's Indifference	18
All is One and One Is All	18
Erato: Muse of Poetry	19
My Dreams	21
Spring's Gown	21
Hope's Breeze	21
The Privilege	22
Smiles and Tears	23
Humanity's Pride	23
I Regret	23
The Book of Life	24
I Wonder . . .	25
Mysterious Life	26
Life	27
Autumn	27
Summer's Crown	27
The Rose	28
The Coming Spring	28
Fire	28
Kissed by the Sun	29
Snowflakes	29
Raindrops	29
Spring	30
Envious Mozart	30
Wrathful Nature	30
Forgive Us, Mother Earth!	31
We and Our Planet	33
Nuptial Gown	34

Table of Contents ... *continued*

Sun's Reign	34
A Mystic Moon	34
Confronting Old Age	35
Cheerful Dawn	36
Man's Epitaph	36
The Sun's Kiss	36
Innocent Youth	37
Resolutions	37

God ... Love ... Faith ... Peace ... Heaven ... Eternity ... Soul   39

The Fragrance	40
Infinite Wisdom	40
The Finest Wine	40
On God's Existence	41
Life's Dawn	43
Fly, My Soul!	43
The Instrument of God	43
In the Name of Fairness	44
Health Is God's Gift	45
God's Glorious Gift	45
Divine Goodness	45
Our Faith	46
The Spark of Faith	46
The Voice of Appreciation	47
In God's Hands	48
The Paris March Against ...	49

Table of Contents ... *continued*

Whispering	51
Love and God	51
The Glorious Star	51
A Fiery Ball	52
Adopted	52
The Sublime World	52
The Sun of Love	52
My Shield	53
Seeking Thee	53
A Chrysalis	53
Wonder Not!	54
His Only Son	54
The Thrills	54
Amendments to Make	55
Father's Love	56
Thanksgiving of the Faithful	56
Defending the Lord	56
Zeus	57
The Soothing Voice	59
An Edifying Life	59
Honor	59
Nous	60
What Really Counts ...	60
Believing or Not	60
Blasphemy	61
Mothers	61
Hades	61
Soul's Sword	62
Inspiration	62

Table of Contents ... *continued*

Pride and Gratitude	62
God's Way and Man's Way	63
Friend or Foe?	64
The Bridge of Peace and Love	65
The Angel and the Soul	65
Friendship	65
Compassion's Voice	66
The Christmas' Star	66
The Most to Gain . . .	66
Our World	67
Tit-for-Tat	67
Veteran's Day	67
Forgive Me, My Lord!	68
Jesus is Born	69
Good Friday	70
Evil Deeds	70
In Strides	70
The Wealthy and the Poor	71
Universal Justice	71
The Mirror	71
Humanity's Shame	72
No Wonder	72

Love ... Romance ... Friendship ... Beauty ... Faithfulness   73

Spring of Love	74
Preposterous	74

Table of Contents ... *continued*

Till Morning Comes	74
No, My Darling . . .	75
Her Smile	75
Her Name to Chant	75
A Blessing or a Curse?	76
Happiness, Unhappiness	76
Divine Eros	76
Eternal Poetry	77
The Richest of Men	77
Wedding Anniversary	77
Betrayal	78
Embraced by Loneliness	78
Trust and Friendship	78
The River of Love	79
Mirage	79
Heavenly Love	80
If Only I Could . . .	80

Knowledge ... Ignorance ... Truth ... Opinion ... Justice ... Politics ... Time   81

The Light of Truth	82
The Circle of Life	82
Love's Womb	83
Cosmic Wisdom	83
Destiny and My Path of Life	84

Table of Contents ... *continued*

Reason and Heart	84
Free Will: Illusion or Reality?	85
Faith's Harbor	89
Yearning for Truth	89
Truthfulness	89
Democracy	90
Voting and Democracy	92
Courting Old Age	92
Editing . . .	93
The Foe	95
Beyond this Valley	95
A Poet's Heart	96
Oxymora	97
Knowing Oneself	98
An Infinite Ocean	99
The Laughs of Youth	99
Good and Evil	100
Man's Character	101
Like Starving Lions	101
The Sparkle of Wisdom	101
Death, My Pal	102
Beastly Appetites	105
The Stranger	106
Knowledge and Wisdom	107
The Deception Queen	107
Unsolved Mystery	107
The Poet and His Muse	108
In Search of Wisdom's Trail	109

Table of Contents ... *continued*

    Lord's Word   109
    No Greater Injustice   110

Author's Quotes   111

Epilogue   121

    about Demetrios Trifiatis   123
    other books Demetrios Trifiatis   127

Acknowledgements

I am grateful to the divine Muse for inspiring my soul to its effort to humbly serve poetry in a miniscule way.

I also thank, with all my heart, Dr. Hülya Yılmaz for her outstanding work in editing and for her continuous support that made this book a reality.

I equally thank William S. Peters, Sr. for his professionalism, generosity and for designing the cover of this book.

Poetic Rapture

Muse's enchanting voice . . .
Whispers of inspiration . . .
Poetic rapture!

Reminder

We
Always ought to
Remember yesterday,
Think of tomorrow
And
Never fail to take care of today,
For
If we don't,
We waste the lessons the past has taught us,
And
We undermine our future!

© Demetrios Trifiatis, January 21st, 2016

Preface

Having lived for more than seven decades on this planet and having traveled extensively around the world;

Having experienced the joys and the sorrows life offers to people and having studied and taught human nature;

Having witnessed our wonderful planet dying slowly and its forests and animals vanishing rapidly

And finally,

Having observed the persistence of Man on walking on the path that, unfailingly, leads to the obliteration of his world and even of his own existence . . .

I have decided to raise my voice and, in my humble way, try to bring to the attention of the reader things that he / she, himself / herself has experienced and learned in his / her passage through life and to ask him / her to join forces so as we, together, fight to avert, if possible, the upcoming catastrophe.

The core of the problem Man faces today, as I perceive it, is a moral one, and that is why we must turn our attention toward it, analyze it once more, and try to offer solutions, no matter what our nationality, creed or color is because we should always remember that the future of humanity is common to each one of us!

The writing of this book is the result of the moral obligation I feel and each one of us ought to feel toward maintaining our Lord's creation, including Man, animals, plants, rivers and oceans. The totality of things though can never be maintained if the condition of the parts is not harmoniously balanced. By the same token, humanity cannot live in peace unless we first have found peace in our hearts.

Only if we all put the common good above the personal one and care for one another, only then could we create a better, kinder, nobler and more loving world. This implies, of course, that we become better, kinder, nobler and more loving ourselves. The answer to all our problems is love! Love toward Man, toward nature, toward animals, toward the totality of things; for, love is unity and unity is God's work. So, let all of us whisper love, for there is no more thunderous voice than the whisper of love!

Demetrios Trifiatis
Ph.D., Philosophy

Author of *Lessons Life Taught Me* and
Co-Author of *An Aegean Breeze of Peace*

Foreword

This book is written for all those who love poetry and have a special place reserved for it in their hearts. However, knowing the author for more than twenty years and being well aware of his academic background in philosophy, I would dare to say that this book is especially written for people who are thirsty for knowledge and are constantly troubling their minds with eternal questions, such as the following: *What is life and what is death? Why are we created and what is the purpose of our existence? Does God exist? What kind of a life should we live and why? What is love, friendship, compassion, peace, justice, war and harmony? How ought we to live and why?*

To me, giving answers to all the questions above is a Herculean task. It is an impossible undertaking for any man to handle, unless, he turns to the inspiring language of poetry and listen to its whispers. Having realized this fact, the author does exactly what is required: Demetrios Trifiatis finds refuge in the language of poetry and he does it brilliantly!

The outcome of his decision is this book, *Whispers of Inspiration* in which he offers us his wonderful poetry that enables our soul to escape the bonds of our egos so as to perceive the world from the higher planes of the spiritual realm. Every verse and every poem of Demetrios Trifiatis awakens our thoughts and feelings, challenging us at the same time, to take a stand. He shares thus his wisdom which springs out of his rich life experience which includes his crossing swords with death in more than one occasion. The result of his encounters with Hades was to perceive the king of the underworld as his pal, his friend, and not as his foe. "Death", says the author, "is a celestial pillow upon which the soul rests for a while dreaming of the life to come." Facing death with equanimity is a sign of wisdom and of acceptance of our mortality which has as a consequence the minimization, even the elimination of our fear of death.

Death is the subject of many of the poems in *Whispers of Inspiration*. The one thought that fascinates me and I consider it to be one of his best poems is the one entitled: "Death, My Pal". I love to read and re-read this poem again and again, for it is so profound and so beautifully written!

In closing my words, I would like to say that we are indebted to you, dear Demetrios, for your superb book that makes us intellectually and emotionally richer!

Alexander Helemskii
Professor and Distinguished Professor of Moscow (Lomonosov) State University
Faculty of Mechanics and Mathematics

Introduction

The new book of Demetrios Trifiatis, *Whispers of Inspiration* shows us that, apart from him being a great poet, he is also an outstanding philosopher – a fact that makes him a highly educated individual in Ancient Greek Letters. This, of course, should not come as a surprise to anyone because Demetrios' academic field is that of philosophy, specifically, in Ethics and Metaphysics which he studied in Canada where he lived, worked and taught for almost twenty years. To the above, I would like to add that he also is a charismatic orator. This trait of the author, I know because I have attended some of his presentations that had enriched my knowledge as well as my feelings.

Demetrios' collections of poems in this book touch a variety of themes that cover all aspects of life: Carnal, mental, sentimental, spiritual and divine. The most important thing for me is that each of his poems carries a specific message and it has a purpose. He wishes to touch our heart, enlighten our mind and uplift our spirit. He puts the emphasis on the moral quality of our life, and although he describes how things are, he always ends up suggesting how things ought to be.

The subjects that he examines are diverse. They start with God and his creation and end with Man and his application of the divine law in everyday life. The values that Demetrios supports and highlights in his poems are universal and touch everyone deeply since they concern themselves with faith, truth, knowledge, virtue, mercy, compassion, harmony, peace, God, eternity after life, and similar universally relevant phenomena.

One good example of the effect his poems have on the reader is his poems related to death. After reading them, one feels liberated from the fear of dying, thus considers death a friend, and not a foe.

Whatever form of poetry Demetrios uses, may it be Rhyme, Quatrain, Haiku, Personification, Narration, Epigrams, Free Verse, Lantern, Acrostic, Monoku or any other form, one thing is certain: He always has something meaningful to share in a very gentle and touching way. His heartfelt feelings for humanity and nature, his profound faith in God, his compassion for the needy and the underprivileged, his adoration of beauty and the divine law fill the reader with warmth, serenity and understanding.

Dear Demetrios, we thank you so much for your hopeful messages and the uplifting sentiments your poems generate in us and fill our hearts and souls. Be blessed and continue doing this excellent, God-loving work you do!

Maria Fragoulopoulou
Professor Emerita
Department of Mathematics
University of Athens, Greece

A Poem Extraordinaire

World Day Against Racism

You asked me the other day, my friend,
Who I am and I replied:
I am you in another body!
Yes, it is true,
Look, how much the same we are,
No matter what the color,
The creed,
The race,
The status.

Look,
I am born and I will die,
I suffer and I enjoy,
I love and I hate,
Just like you.

I am a father, a brother, a son,
A mother, a sister, a daughter,
Just like you.

Happiness, I seek,
Family to raise is my wish,
Peace to find I look for,
Just like you.

I yearn.
I abhor.

I fear.
I hope.

I bleed.
I heal.
Just like you.

I believe.
I doubt.

I accept.
I refuse.

I laugh.
I cry.
Just like you.

We are alike.
We are the same.
We are brothers . . .

Children of a unique father.

Tell me,
My brother,
My friend,
My ally,
Why do we have to oppose,
To fight,
To hurt,
To destroy and
To eliminate
One another?

Are our seas really that narrow,
Our oceans that small,
Our lands so limited
To contain all of us?

Or
Is it the case that
Our hearts are not big enough
And our minds not so wide-open

To enfold all mankind?
Listen to me, my other self:
It is up to us to change this world
We have inherited with its virtues and vices,
History and culture,
Flaws and merits
And try to make it
Better,
Nobler,
Kinder and more caring
By obliterating harmful beliefs,
Demolishing injurious divisions,
Destroying detrimental distrust,
Annihilating racism and eradicating
The erroneous feeling of poisonous superiority
To bring the dawn of a new loving world,
A world of acceptance,
Of respect,
Of justice,
Of equality,
Of love and
Of universal brotherhood

So as
With peace in our hearts, liberated we would be
From the past's deleterious tribulations
That for a myriad of years
Have kept us fighting one another!

© Demetrios Trifiatis
March 21, 2015

"World Day Against Racism"

On the 21st of March of 2015, I have written the poem that appears here with the same title, and posted it on one of the most sizeable online poetry groups of global endeavors in which I have been a "Premium Member" since August 2012. As the site's first non-American writer, I have posted over 2300 poems on that platform where I have been designated as one of the most prolific poets.

"World Day Against Racism" has been distinguished on the above-mentioned poetry venue as one of its one hundred best poems ever written. The ensued interest for it was, as I conclude now, one of the reasons as to why one of the most prominent academic research organizations in the U.S. has selected it as a worthy project.

This poem is the result of many negative experiences I have had throughout my life: As an orphan, as a poor, as a villager and as an immigrant in a foreign land. These experiences encouraged me to work with humanitarian and peace organizations so as to help eradicate the wrong-doings in this world. Even my education in philosophy was due to my desire to fight against racism and all forms of discriminations that we see in our everyday lives.

The representative of the highly prestigious academic research organization of my previous mention is associated with a renowned university in the USA wished to create a video program that promotes the equality among people, regardless of their race, creed, nationality, sex or sexual orientation. She has chosen my poem, "World Day Against Racism" as an inspiration in order to incarnate the ideal of equality. She contacted me last July and asked for my permission and collaboration. My permission was happily given, and I have enthusiastically collaborated with the said representative so as the desired goal could be achieved.

Now that the efforts of many people have reached fruition, a documentary is being created of which the premier will take place soon after the publication of this book at a venue that the host academic organization will indicate. I will be attending this event as an invited speaker. The specific details will be distributed to the public by the involved academic constituents.

Demetrios Trifiatis

Whispers of Inspiration

Demetrios Trifiatis

Whispers Of Inspiration

The Poetry

Whispers Of Inspiration

Life

Man

Destiny

Nature

Environment

Cosmos

Once Born

Once born, death is our lot.
When we die: Immortality!

All I Am

All I am, oh life,
To the relentless battering
Of your storms I owe!

Life's Sailing

Life's boat is sailing
On the turbulent dark seas . . .
Rudder, in God's hands!

Forgiving Life

I forgive you, oh life
For the myriads of tears of grief
You made me shed
Only because you gave my heart
The chance to love!

The Rising Sun

Good morning rising sun, the king of the sky!
What you have in store for me today, I ignore.
However, one thing I wish so much to know:
Would I be still there at your sunset to adore?

The Dream

Life:
A dream
Expecting
To come true in
Death!

Walking Under the Sun

Walking under the morning's bright sun
Its kind rays and I tenderly embrace,
Saying, life a gentle stroll should be
Not a strenuous marathon race!

Swimming Upstream

My soul has left the serene ocean of the eternal
And like a salmon, swims upstream
The river's turbulent waters of the temporal,
Determined to overcome any obstacles found
For its destiny to fulfill!

An Eventful Life

To you, oh fates, I pray:
A short but eventful life to grant me to live
Rather than a long uneventful one to enjoy!

Cosmic Dance

What are we but dancers of the cosmic order,
Obliged to dance our life away,
To dance our death away?

Few steps we may learn at times
As we advance in age,
But we have never enough time
Our dancing to improve,
Let alone to perfect it.
For the choreography is infinite
And we, alas, so temporal
While the heavens' choreographer
So demanding

Demetrios Trifiatis

The Breath of Life

Don't ask, my friend
How much of His breath our Lord
Has breathed into each of us*!
If a cubic millimeter it is
Or a cubic decimeter,
For it doesn't matter at all
Since HE is infinite,
And the infinite divided by any number,
Infinite remains
Thus, into you and me, His infinity has breathed.
So, by following His Word,
You and I, my brother, my sister,
With the passing of time, perfect we are able to be
As our Father in heaven is perfect
In His holy ways!**

*Genesis 2:7
**Matthew 5:48

Whispers Of Inspiration

Once upon A Time . . .

This is Zeus*, the life-giving God speaking:

Come, come all you blind forces!
Come out of chaos!

Let us bring order,
So out of this anarchy
A cosmos to be born,
A cosmos where uniformity will reign
And the Law of my Logos will be obeyed by all.

To achieve this though, you all have to learn how to dance,
To dance the dance of peaceful coexistence,
But first, a partner for you I shall find.

Now, all pay attention!
Here is the list I have prepared for you:

Accord dances with discord,
Unity with division,
Love with hate,
Joy with sorrow,
Hope with despair,
Pleasure with suffering,
Harmony with strife,
Mind with matter,
Hot with cold,
Humid with arid,
Hard with soft . . .
And the temporal with the eternal!

Be careful now!
For each step you take, your partner will take one.
Keep in mind that you don't dance alone.

Demetrios Trifiatis

Respect your dancing partner, and he will respect you.

What we try to achieve here is harmony.
Only then this wondrous choreography
Of creation will be successful.

There you are!
Slowly, dance back and forth, listening
To this wondrous symphony of life.

Thus, spoke Zeus and managed to unite the opposites
which resulted in the world we live in!

*Greek Mythology tells us that when Zeus decided to create the world, he turned himself into Eros (God of love) so as to be able to unite the opposite forces that existed within the Chaos in order to give birth to a harmonious Cosmos.

Poetry

Poetry
Sees the unseen,
Hears the unheard,
Comprehends the incomprehensible . . .

Praises our feelings,
Exalts our love,
Glorifies our God . . .

Describes nature,
Expresses beauty,
Gives wings to inspiration.

Poetry,
The heavenly language
That the devotees of the Muses use
To paint reality as our Lord
Meant reality to be:
Divine!

Flowers

F--- Felicitous
   L--- Luminous
      O--- Ornaments
         W--- Whispering
            E--- Enchanting
               R--- Romantic
                  S--- Songs!

My Odyssey

Here, I am . . .
Retired,
Happy,
Sitting on the relaxing throne of my age,
Reminiscing what I went through in life.
A mere spectator I have now become,
Observing in silence the works of men,
Having no worries of
Carrier advancement,
Of acceptance,
Of recognition . . .

Free at last!
Liberated I feel from all of the soul-disturbing
Situations that preoccupy humans all life-long
In order to enable themselves to survive.

When young,
Things were different . . .
As I wanted to change things,
I roamed the world, visiting all continents but one.
Myriad of dreams I had, each demanding to be realized.

From my part, I did my best despite life's hardships . . .
Starting with the loss of both of my parents
When I was in my early teens . . .
Then, poverty came, and orphanage.
The intensified struggle for survival – working
And studying, being alone at the age of fifteen
Is not a laughing matter!
Afterward, I served in the army,
Became a track-and-field athlete,
Immigrated to Canada.

Knowing no-one over there,
Speaking little English and having no money . . .
Life was a living hell for a long period of time,
But slowly things turned around,
For Canada is a great country,
It gave me the chance to work
And the opportunity to study.

I started working during the day,
Going to the university in the evening,
Learned English, French and German,
Did my undergraduate studies, and then
Completed my post-graduate studies,
Started teaching,
Had my own philosophical TV and Radio program
In three languages at a community station,
Became an author,
Got married,
Had a daughter.

Eighteen years later, I found myself back in Greece . . .
I directed different schools and private colleges and
In collaboration with professors from Athens University,
Helped to organize international conferences on
Philosophy, religion, politics, education and peace.
Afterward, out of moral obligations,
I was involved in politics and ran, six times in total,
For the Greek and the European parliament
With no success.
I did humanitarian work, consoling people,
Visiting hospitals, mental institutions, and
Under the auspices of the Greek Ministry of Justice,
Prisons – high security ones included . . .
Life obligated me to meet people of all walks of life:
Poor men and women that had nothing at all,

Demetrios Trifiatis

Rich and the very rich that had everything,
The illiterate that could not read or write as well as
Famous professors and writers.
Moreover, I met politicians:
Members of the parliament,
Ministers,
Prime Ministers and
Presidents of different countries.
Also, I came in contact with religious men
Of many denominations:
Bishops,
Archbishops,
Patriarchs, Mullahs
But also, many criminals:
Thieves, rapists, murderers, including some who
Had committed fratricide, matricide and patricide.

I had a harsh and at times torturous life
But never a boring one . . .
I was born in an occupied country
During the second World War, and lived
The first five years while a civil war was raging.

If one would ever ask me to live my life again,
My reply would be a thunderous NO!
I could not take it anymore.
Unless . . .
It was to live it again for a higher purpose,
Such as to help achieve world peace.

If one asks me what beautifies life, without hesitation,
I would say: LOVE and LEARNING.

If one makes inquiries from where

I drew the strength to overcome all hardships,
I would say, my unshakable faith in God
Who adopted me after the death of my parents,
And my undying love for my fellow man.

If one wishes to know,
What is the most difficult thing in life, my reply will be:
To accept life as well as to accept oneself.
Now, in the degree we do not accept life or ourselves,
We suffer!
If one insists on finding out
What is important for any person in life,
The answer for me is, "To know himself, to be truthful
To himself and to do the best he can by using
The abilities our Lord has provided him with.
That means it is preferable to be a fine butcher than a lousy surgeon!

Finally,
One should never fear death for the simple reason:
None is exempted!
Death for me is a celestial pillow
Upon which the soul rests for a while,
Dreaming of the life to come.
Life much resembles the sea which, either turbulent or calm, has the same depth.

Accept life, and in time, one may learn
How to face death with equanimity!
I am at that point now, with no regrets, other than
I could have learned more
And have done more in my life.

I thank God for each day I have lived as I thank

Demetrios Trifiatis

All those who, directly or indirectly, have enriched
My life's experience and have helped me
Live this adventure, including all of you
Who are reading these lines now!

God bless each and every one of you
To follow your Destiny's path with
Courage, love and faith in your heart!

One's Indifference

One's indifference
Toward the advancement of evil
Condemns the soul to a perpetual state
Of moral stagnation and guilt!

All Is One and One Is All

All is One and One is All,
For the One gives birth to All
And the All adds up to the One
According to God's immutable laws.
Thus, whoever commits a crime against the part,
Undoubtedly commits a crime against the whole.
So, the universal justice steps in
To punish the transgressor
For harmony to reestablish itself
And for God's law to be maintained!

Erato: Muse of Poetry

Uninvited you come, oh Erato*, Muse of poetry . . .
The majority of times, knocking at my soul's door
At any given moment, insisting to let you in,
Your message to deliver, disregarding
At what state my soul is
And if she could, indeed,
With your request comply . . .

Oh, Muse of poetry, when with my soul's inspiration
You constantly flirt, whispering into her ears words
Of wisdom, coming from your divine essence,
My soul, mesmerized, tries the words of
Wisdom that have been lingering in her
Depths, again to remember.

A difficult task it is indeed, I admit,
For the language of heavens
That my soul once knew well,
She must now remember
Through her association
With her mortal body.
For that reason, oh divine Muse,
Be patient with her
And give her just
A little more time
To reconsider!

The time that my soul needs, divine Muse,
Is to learn or rather, to remember how to talk
And to express herself in writing the way you would like:
In accordance with the universe's harmony
And its eternal laws.

When this blessed hour comes,

Able would my soul be
Inspiring poems to compose . . .
But for her writings, her creations and her poetic epics,
The work of you, oh Muse, no credit would my soul claim,
For she knows very well that she is only an instrument,
Oh Muse, into your godly embrace, just to be used
According to your guidance . . .
Because only you, oh Muse of poetry, know how
The universe's poetic language should be used
And how, in verse, it has to be delivered!

Erato, one of the nine daughters of Zeus and Mnemosyne (memory), is the Muse of lyric poetry, love poetry and marriage songs.

My Dreams

Dreams drifted me off
Reality, left behind
Endless freedom found!

Spring's Gown

Bright vibrant colors
Reviving nature's canvas,
Spring's new-fashioned gown!

Hope's Breeze

Hope's breeze
Filled the sails of my dreams
And carried me over the vast seas
Of the unknown in search of
My destiny's shores
Of realization!

The Privilege

The dawn arrived
And I am still here,

    Standing
        Breathing
            Watching
                Listening
                    Touching
                        Scenting
                            Tasting
                        Admiring
                    Wondering
                Enjoying
            Exclaiming
          Celebrating
    Praying

And offering thanksgivings
To our Lord for the unique privilege
That so many have lost: TO BE ALIVE!

Smiles and Tears

Smiles
God gave
To humans
To absorb grief's
Tears!

Humanity's Pride

Children's life at risk . . .
Slumbering planet awakes
Humanity's pride!

I Regret

As my life's days are getting shorter with age
And darkness seems slowly to weave the night,
I regret the light so thoughtlessly wasted
When youth's sun had shined endlessly so bright!

The Book of Life

The book of one's life has been written.
The paths one has to walk on have been traced.
The goals to be achieved have been chosen.
The time of completion of the events has been set.
One has just to read carefully and understand
The plot of this book, walk on the indicated paths
And never deviate from them, help materialize
Each of the goals according to one's abilities,
And finally, be ready to accept what may come . . .
Without complaining.
Our Lord has given each of us
What it takes to constructively partake
Of the becoming of the cosmic order.
He neither coerces us nor allows us
His divine plans to destroy.
He has given us freedom,
But . . . He has also set
Inviolable universal laws
To safeguard His creation.
Thus, whoever oversteps these cosmic laws
Will face the consequences of His actions.
In that case, one has to know
That God is not to be blamed!

I Wonder . . .

I wonder,
If ever the fruit thanks the tree
For helping it grow and becoming ripe;

I wonder,
If the tree ever thanks its roots
For keeping it standing and for the nourishment
It provides;

I wonder,
If ever the roots thank the ground
For supplying a firm base to plant themselves
In search of food;

I wonder,
If ever the ground thanks the microorganisms and minerals
For enriching its soil so as to become alive . . .

If no one ever expresses gratitude to each other,
Then a great injustice is committed
UNLESS . . .
All of the above is one,
And as such, all work in unison for a single purpose:
To serve the divine will to maintain life!

Mysterious Life

Life:
    This drama
        This mystery
            This enigma
                This paradox
                    This choreography
                    This symphony
                        This phantasmagoria
                        This poetry
                          This ecstasy
                              This apotheosis of
                              Creation . . .
Let us embrace it with all our heart and mind,
For humanity in harmony to live, and us, God to glorify!

Life

Life:
An endless battle fought
Between
Spirit and matter,
Truth and falsity,
Heaven and Earth,
The temporal and the eternal
From dawn till dusk,
From the cradle to the grave
And BEYOND!

Autumn

Summer's memories,
Inscribed on golden old leaves.
Paved is winter's path!

Summer's Crown

Winter, forgotten.
Sunbeams undress the cloudy sky.
Summer claims its crown!

The Rose

The rose, I asked:
"Why a tender flower like you
is armed with so many thorns?"

"Because there are as many unfeeling foes
lurking around", it bitterly replied!

The Coming Spring

The chilling morning breeze caressed the yet-asleep
    frozen ground

Whispering in its passage the joyous message
    of the coming Spring

Awakening thus Earth's desires, imprisoned
    in winter's dungeon,

Which, liberated, in the fields of myriad flower hues,
    sanctuary found!

Fire

A hellish fire came.
Hopes and dreams burned to the ground.
Souls flew in terror!

Kissed by the Sun

Half-blooming flowers,
Tenderly kissed by the sun.
Nature's magic show!

Snowflakes

Winter's frozen tears
Scattered on the despairing ground
Sparkling diamonds!

Raindrops

Raindrops are falling,
Whispering heaven's secrets.
Rejoiced is my soul!

Spring

S-Spectacular
   P-Plants'
      R-Rebirth
         I-Initiating
            N-Nature's
               G-Glorification!

Envious Mozart

Morning's breeze is filled
With melodious Spring sounds.
Envious Mozart!

Wrathful Nature

Wrathful trilogy:
Typhoons, cyclones, hurricanes
Stern warning to Man!

Forgive Us, Mother Earth!

For decades now,
We, your children, dear Mother Earth,
Have been stabbing you
Each year,
Each month,
Each day,
Each hour,
Each minute and
Each second,
Causing you to bleed profusely,
While
We, indifferent to your suffering, have been
Watching,
Laughing,
Drinking,
Dancing and
Having fun,
For we thought your blood was inexhaustible,
That you would bleed forever,
Without any consequence on
Our own life, but slowly,
We came to realize that you are as mortal as we are,
Subject to the same laws of decay,
A shocking thought this was indeed for us!
However,
In spite of this realization
We never stopped hurting
You,
Your animals,
Your forests,
Your rivers,
Your lakes,
Your seas,
Your oceans.

You see, dear Mother Earth,
We have sacrificed all you have held dear
For millions of years to the altar of our
Egoism and that of our vanity.

Now,
As we see you lie in your death-bed,
We, your conceited and spoiled children,
Have decided to give you a last chance
To stop your bleeding, to end your torture and your
Agony so as to give you time to recover.

Yes, we know,
Our action is not out of magnanimity or of love for you,
But mainly out of fear we might destroy
Our blasphemous species
That for centuries
Has overstepped
The limits
That our Lord has set from the moment of His creation
For that, I for one, on my knees, humbly plead
For your forgiveness for my participation
In this horrid and macabre crime
Of matricide!

We and Our Planet

Creation
  Maturation
    Adaptation
      Proliferation
        Evolution
          Industrialization
            Automation
              Production
                Pollution
                  Suffocation
                    Destruction
                      Obliteration
                          Man's Extinction?
                            Planet's salvation!

Nuptial Gown

Snowfall:
Dancing nymphs
Of Winter's soul
Masterfully weaving
Nature's nuptial gown!

Sun's Reign

Sun's reign was over.
The scepter passed to night's hands.
Stars envied the throne!

A Mystic Moon

A mystic moon lit the sky.
Light set sea's face on fire.
Ladder to heaven!

Confronting Old Age

I see you coming, old age,
Approaching at an ever-accelerating pace,
Your face so grim
Your expression so austere,
Your look so menacing.
A frightening sight you are!

Many battles have I fought in my life
With vigor and youth by my side,
Thus, victorious I emerged.

But . . .

Now that my allies slowly abandon me
One after the other,
I am left alone the last battle to fight,
A battle, I know beforehand,
I am bound to lose.

However . . .

At this moment as trials begin
When all seem to get tougher by the day,
A new ally have I found, willing to help me,
All my courage to amass for to confront you.
Oh, merciless old age:
The wisdom I have acquired all these years
Roaming the planes of experience and learning!

Cheerful Dawn

Dawn, I met a few minutes ago.
Anxious was she into the light the world to bathe,
So we humans another day to enjoy.

"Tell me, oh glorious Dawn," I asked:
"How do you manage so cheerful each morning to be
when Man's crimes against other men and against
nature you witness every day?"

Smiling, she looked at me and so replied:
"My mission is not to judge anyone or anything
but only the night's darkness to chase away!"

Man's Epitaph

Here lies Man – a species of certain wit
Who with great success did the atom split,
But that knowledge he misused.
For he was always confused,
Destroyed himself. For he did never quit!

The Sun's Kiss

The Sun kissed dark clouds.
Dissipated was their gloom.
Flowers jumped for joy!

Innocent Youth

Oh, tender youth,
I terribly regret the crimes humanity
Upon your innocent shoulders has placed!

Resolutions

R-Revived
  E-Expectations
    S-Specifying
      O-Optimistic
        L-Life
          U-Undertakings
            T-To
              I-Incarnate
                O-Omitted
                  N-Noble
                    S-Solutions!

Whispers Of Inspiration

God

Love

Faith

Peace

Heaven

Eternity

Soul

The Fragrance

Invisible like a flower's fragrance God is,
Yet amply known His presence He makes!

Infinite Wisdom

Lord's wisdom, one should never judge,
For infinite are the things that Man ignores!

The Finest Wine

Yes, I confess!
Intoxicated I am with life
For its finest wine I have drunk:
Love!

On God's Existence

What am I?
Am I just matter?
Am I just spirit?
Or am I a combination
Of spirit and matter?

If we examine the first case – that I am matter,
Then it follows that whatever I am, I have borrowed it
From nature to use it for a while and then return it in its
Totality to nature to be used once more
By something or someone else.

It is clear, therefore, that as far as matter is concerned,
What I am already existed in nature in a different form:
A fruit,
A plant,
A mineral,
An animal,
For nature loves to recycle its matter eternally,
Since the law of conservation of energy
Is applicable to the whole of the universe
And it is everlasting!

Now, following the argument established here,
We have to agree that whatever is in the part
Is also in the total, although the totality of a thing
Could never be in a part of it.
In other words, whatever a drop of water is,
It is part of the water, contained in the lake,
In the sea or in the ocean, but the totality
Of the water in the lake, sea or the ocean
Could never be contained
in the drop of the water.
Having adopted this line of argument . . .

Whenever something exists in the part, it means
That it pre-existed in the total, otherwise the part
Could never be what it is. For, it would have been
Self-created, without any help from outside – things
That we know to be impossible!

Now, to continue this line of thought,
A further step we have to take:
Since I am what I am, materially always speaking, I realize
Instantly that I am something more than matter. For, I am
Conscious of what surrounds me. Moreover, I feel and
I also am thinking . . . for this to occur, certainly, proves
That something in the universe, long time before me, was
Able to feel and also was thinking . . .
Otherwise, I myself as a part of the whole could never had
Properties that had not existed before I become alive
And conscious enough to ask questions like the ones
I am asking now.

This reasoning leads us directly to the conclusion that
The universe must be conscious, which means that it feels
And also, that it is thinking. Therefore, a being
With properties that have been described above,
Is existing, and this being could be called God.
For, God is the consciousness of the totality of things,
And at the same time, is present in each existing thing
That allows Him to create the world in His own image:
Matter and spirit harmoniously collaborating and coexisting
For life to exist for an eschatological divine purpose that,
Alas, to us mortals would never be revealed in its totality!

Life's Dawn

Thy word, my Lord, life's dawn brings.
Thy blessings make the cosmos shine.
Thy love every heart with faith fills.
Creation's symphony divine!

Fly, My Soul!

Fly
My soul,
Ascend high.
On heaven's ground,
Walk!

The Instrument of God

Man: God's instrument
Double nature – body, soul
Seeking harmony!

In the Name of Fairness

Alone he stood against the many,
A towering rock of integrity,
Unafraid,
Uncompromising,
Determined to fight in the name of
The weak and the poor that victims to
Greedy persons' unholy and devious plans have fallen.

Ready was he to struggle against these
Insatiable men and the injustices they committed, till
Things changed, and fairness was restored,
For he knew in his heart of hearts that
The forces of
Good,
Justice
And of virtue stood by his side,
Stronger by far
Than any of their deceitful armies of conspirators and
Their evil schemes to support inequity.
For, to glorify greed's contemptible vanity,
Remaining indifferent to the suffering they inflicted
Upon all those who their trust had put in them,
Expecting a fair play!
Shame!

Health Is God's Gift

Health is God's most precious gift of value untold
That is more precious than all diamonds and gold.

As long as we possess it, we seem not to care
But as soon as we lose it, we find it unfair.

Better would be for us health more to appreciate,
Thanksgiving offer to God and life celebrate!

God's Glorious Gift

His birthday arrived.
God's glorious gift received.
Life's celebration!

Divine Goodness

Oh, divine goodness that resides in Man's heart,
The time has come for you the world to prepare,
As with your love, truth, values and compassion
Each human being that lives to be aware!

Our Faith

Our unwavering faith in the Lord,
An inexhaustible power it is
That our compassionate deeds propel,
Blessed by divinity's mighty breeze!

The Spark of Faith

The spark of faith in my heart
Ignited my slumbering courage
Which grew to a wild blaze
And consumed every doubt
And every obstacle
That existed in my mind,
Thus, allowed me, my Lord,
To achieve the goals,
Thee had set for me
Since the beginning of time!

The Voice of Appreciation

My dearest troubled humans,
This is the bitter voice of Appreciation of old
That you are hearing, the one that, once upon a time,
People much revered, but the younger generations
Seem not even to know my name.

I remember when all of you had my name on your lips,
When children constantly appreciated
What their parents, for them, were doing;
Students were thankful for what their teachers,
For them, were teaching;
Citizens were grateful for what their state,
For them, was providing;
People were offering thanksgivings to God
For taking care of their needs,
And statues were erected everywhere in my honor.
Now, my name, as though forbidden to be pronounced,
Obliterated from your memory, it appears to be.
Thus, all and each one of you, only to yourselves
Give credit, forgetting that without the contributions
Of those that came before you, you yourselves
Wild animals would be, lacking language,
Sciences and numbers . . .
Just ignorant brutes, striving in the wilderness,
Struggling to survive.

Beware, my beloved humans,
On the road of ingratitude
You keep following for long,
Sooner than later,
Back in the wilderness,
Your egotistic selves, inescapably,
You would find!

In God's Hands

Here I am, my Lord,
Falling . . .
Without a parachute,
For I have faith
In my heart
That no harm
Will ever come to me
Since my life
Is in Thy hands!

The Paris March Against the Beast of Fear

The raging beast of fear in darkness was conceived.
Its father: Terror.
Its mother: Ignorance.
With the black milk of hate was it breastfed.
By wrath was it nurtured.
By fanaticism was its character forged,
And its soul was saturated with repugnance.

Thus . . .

The deformed prince of gloom, once matured,
A menace to humanity it grew up to be,
Threatening the beacon of civilization to extinguish by
Terrorizing,
Torturing,
Burning,
Raping,
Enslaving,
Decapitating,
Executing . . .
All this, in the name of a God that the brute
Doesn't even understand.
So, it demanded the whole world to kneel in dread.

BUT . . .

Humanity didn't succumb.
United, in its finest hour, it marched on,
Unyielding,
Unafraid,
Uncompromising,
Proud and

Free,
Sending thus the message to the kingdom of gloom
That its days are numbered.
For . . .

One ray of light, mightier is than any amount of darkness
And easily could obliterate the beast's obscure empire
At a blink of the eye.

Because . . .

GOD is not HATE and DARKNESS,
But LIGHT and LOVE!

Whispering

God's whispers I heard.
My eyes saw His reflection.
Soul's Enlightenment!

Love and God

Love
Places us
Next to our
Benevolent
God!

The Glorious Star

The glorious star of Your Word, my Lord,
Led my soul onto the constellation of your wisdom!

A Fiery Ball

A fiery ball of pure consciousness our soul is,
Gathering wisdom's stardust throughout eternity!

Adopted

Parents passed away.
Orphan, early he was left.
By God he was adopted!

The Sublime World

The steed of spirit I mounted,
And galloped to the end of time.
Passing through the eras of reality,
Reached I the world sublime!

The Sun of Love

Once more, Christ is born.
The sun of love has risen.
Cloudless is the sky!

My Shield

Here I am my Lord,
Standing tall,
Unafraid,
Facing the forces of evil,
Regardless how strong they might be,
For Thou Word,
My shield I have made!

Seeking Thee

All my life, I was seeking Thee my Lord,
Before I realized
That Thee had me already found!

A Chrysalis

A chrysalis is my soul, oh Lord,
Striving a butterfly to be,
To Thy realm to fly!

Wonder Not!

Wonder neither where your soul comes from
Nor to where it goes,
As it knows its holy path to follow,
For into divinity's river it flows!

His Only Son

Unrepentant hearts forever nails become for Christ
 to crucify,
But God's love for us, his only son sacrifices so
 death to defy.

The Thrills

My immortal soul I asked:
"Why have you chosen to incarcerate yourself
within the walls of perishable flesh?"
"To witness the thrills of the temporary",
was her for me-surprising reply!

Amendments to Make

The last moment of his life came,
The one beyond anxiously awaited
To receive him into its eternal embrace.
He was terrified!

He asked for some more time,
Wished some amendments to make:
Wrong doings to make right,
To give love to those he hated,
To help those in need,
To be truthful to those he betrayed,
To ask forgiveness from those he hurt . . .
Alas!
Adamant was the Lord of the hereafter:
"Such requests can never be gratified", he said,
"You see, the law of cause and effect is unforgiving.
the balance of things should be maintained. Otherwise, the
harmony of the whole would be disturbed", he added.
"What you sow is what you reap",
With emphasis he declared.
"Do not worry though," he continued,
"On this side, absolute justice prevails,
for it is irrelevant if one is a king or a beggar.
Thus, you will receive the right sentence, but always
with the agreement of your soul – God's ambassador in you
that, unenforced, will offer the final accurate testimony
of your actions on Earth, adding nothing
and subtracting nothing", he concluded!

Father's Love

Incarnated as a man,
His father's love to us brought.
Crucifixion, his reward.
Heavenly Glory!

Thanksgiving of the Faithful

"Humbly, I thank Thee, oh Lord
For considering my fleeting being
A necessary part of Thy glorious Creation!"
The faithful exclaimed!

Defending the Lord

With all my might,
I will defend Thee, my Lord,
From the blasphemous.
For, I know in my heart of hearts
Thou art is holy!

Zeus

Oh Zeus,
Ruler of starry heavens and of fertile Earth,
Supreme among Gods and father of all men!
Thy name is known to me, although Thy essence
Unknown to me remains.
For, no mortal, since time was born, has set eyes upon
Thy Divine image,
But Thee, immortal God, through the millennia
With different names to mortals have appeared.
Nonetheless, immutable and undeniable, forever you stay!

Zeus, the "life-giver", Thee are called,
But too many of us have chosen with a different name
Thee to identify.
So, I implore Thee, not to be offended if
By a diverse name I call Thee,
Because my action doesn't spring out of disrespect
Or spite but is rather the result of my ignorance,
And intention, I have none to diminish Thy Holy substance.

Tell me, oh mighty Zeus,
Why in Thy name, throughout history,
People have been constantly killing one another?
This is difficult for me to understand, as you,
The father of all of us were, are and would always be.
So, how could it ever be possible for Thee
From one of your children to demand
Another of yours to slay?

Only one thing, I beg Thee oh Zeus, God of Gods
And of all the peoples' father:
Is it feasible ever to enlighten us, the ignorant,
Of your divine essence,
Of your immutability,

Omniscience,
Goodness and omnipotence,
For us to be able to see and comprehend that Thee
This world has out of love created
And that Thou law is eternal,
For us to be convinced from now on
Peacefully to live in harmonious coexistence?

The Soothing Voice

I leave the bustling-with people-city
And the roaring traffic that I much fear
To run to the woods of placid country
The soothing voice of my Lord to hear!

An Edifying Life

An edifying life we all ought to live
With each thought, word and deed
If we wish a better world to make and to follow
Our Lord's divine creed!

Honor

Live
Our life
With honor
Till the hour we
Die!

Nous

Oh Nous,
You, divine faculty of perception,
Mother of conception,
Source of understanding,
Gate of wisdom!
Without your presence, deaf and blind I would be,
Perpetually oblivious to truth eternal.

What Really Counts . . .

For our Lord,
It is not the number of days
We live on Earth that counts,
But the number of days
We devote to manifest His will:
To Love!

Believing or Not

Believing in God or not,
Accountable we all are for our actions the same.
We must keep that well in our mind,
For we are not going to evade the blame.

Blasphemy

Cosmic harmony:
God's infinite creation.
Blasphemous humans.

Mothers

God
Creates
Our mothers
To incarnate
Love!

Hades

Death I saw passing by my neighborhood
The other day, some souls to harvest.
Intrigued by his austere appearance,
I approached him and asked:
"Why, oh you mighty Hades,
by your presence we mortals are terrified?"
"Because of your ignorance", he enigmatically replied.

*Hades, brother of Zeus, Lord of the underworld.

Soul's Sword

Faith:
Soul's sword,
Doubt's slayer,
Champion of God!

Inspiration

Muse's tune resonates.
Poet, melody composes.
Verses' symphony!

Pride and Gratitude

The fool's heart is filled just with pride for his achievements,
While mostly with gratitude is filled the heart of the wise!

God's Way and Man's Way

A seed was planted.
It took roots.
A tree grew out of it,
Which thousands of seeds produced
That fell on the ground.
Soon, an impenetrable forest appeared.
That is God's way of doing things.

The Word of the Lord was transmitted.
Millions of ears heard the message.
Alas! Only a few hearts allowed it
To take roots in them and even fewer
Were willing to spread the Word,
Thus, endangering it to disappear
Into oblivion.
That is Man's way!

Friend or Foe?

Oh, mighty Death,
Undisputed ruler of the underworld,
Tell me, I implore you,
Are you my friend or my foe?
Are you the dark angel or the angel of light?
Should I fear you or should I rejoice at your sight?

During my long life, I know,
We have crossed paths a good number of times.
There were moments that face to face we came.
At other times, you, like a serpent, were lurking unseen
In the grass of my fears.

As a mortal, undoubtedly to you I belong,
But still my question lingers:
When the time comes, am I bound your prisoner to be
Or your guest of honor?

The Bridge of Peace and Love

No land or sea would ever be so vast
To prevent us, my dear brother, my caring sister,
From building the blessed
By heaven's bridge of peace and love
That humanity for centuries now yearns to construct
So that, after so many millennia of painful separation,
Able would we into each-other's arms us to throw!

The Angel and the Soul

An angel, in his heavenly tranquility,
Observing the lamentations of an inconsolable soul
Because of its upcoming incarceration
Within the walls of mortal flesh,
Turned toward it and said calmly:
"Be patient, dear soul, for manifold
your rewards will be
for such a sacrifice!"

Friendship

Bliss's sanctified tears,
Heaven's blessed rain of love:
Friendship eternal!

Compassion's Voice

Helping the poor, the needy, the lonely
Is the way that love makes one's heart rejoice,
For it knows Jesus would incarnate only
If humanity hears compassion's voice!

The Christmas Star

Oh, you Christmas star in the dark sky above,
Ignite our hearts with the spark of divine love
For our souls to be blessed by the Lord's grace
So as greed holy compassion will replace!

The Most to Gain . . .

No, my beloved brother,
As enemies we were never born
But made so by all those vicious men
That had the most to gain!

Our World

Our world, a holy world and an evil world it is
Where the best and the worst of people one may find,
People willing their own lives for others to give
While others kill for not having a heart that is kind!

Tit-for-Tat

Tit-for-tat,
A philosophy that humanity
Has never been able to combat!

Veteran's Day

Oh, you blessed souls that for us have fallen,
We wish the loftiest of appreciations
For your sacrifice to show
By thanking you for the opportunity
Given to us to enjoy
The greatest gift of all which you have missed:
LIFE!

Forgive Me, My Lord!

On my knees,
Humbly, I Thee implore, my Lord
To forgive me, your foolish servant
For complaining for having not the things
I desired:
The color of eyes I wished for,
The gorgeous ears,
The lovely nose,
The fine-looking hands,
The straight legs,
The stunning body,
Instead of thanking Thee
For what to me Thou have given:
Eyes that can Thy creation see,
Ears that enable me Thy melodies to enjoy,
A nose that nature's aromas permit me scent,
Hands that allow me to touch and to caress,
Legs that permit me to move about, and finally,
A healthy body – swift and strong
That functioned well for such a long time.

Show Thy mercy, my Lord, I Thee beseech
Because I have failed to sooner realize
The worth of all Thy divine gifts!

Jesus Is Born

In the middle of the night you came, sweet Jesus,
To bring us light, in winter, to bring us warmth.
Of the manger you were born
To teach us humility.
On an impoverished land you grew
To distribute your spiritual wealth.
Of war you marched
To bring us peace.
On an occupied land you chose to live
To bring us freedom.
Humanity's condemnation
You placed upon yourself
To lead us into salvation.
To hatred you opened yourself
To instruct us how to love!

We pray to you, divine infant,
Our weary hearts to purify
So as worthy we would be
Your Holy name to glorify!

Good Friday

Into Hades Man descended
  Darkness dissipated
    Death eliminated
      Man liberated:
        JESUS!

Evil Deeds

The deeds of an evil man
The work of a myriad good men could destroy,
But no matter what he achieves,
The Lord's love unable would he be to enjoy.

In Strides

In strides, evil walks.
Good has been left far behind.
Sorrowfulness' joy!

The Wealthy and the Poor

Billions of poor suffer.
Few greedy men enjoy wealth.
Humanity's crime!

Universal Justice

Beware, my mortal friends,
For there is
No thought,
No sentiment,
No feeling,
No intention,
No word and,
Certainly, no action of ours
That would ever be possible
To escape the discernment of
Universal justice!

The Mirror

Human consciousness . . .
Mirror of the eternal.
Reflection, missing!

Humanity's Shame

Starving children die.
Peacefully, the greedy sleep.
Humanity's shame!

No Wonder

No wonder, for Man, peace in the heart is difficult to find.
For, cosmic strife in his soul has succeeded deeply to hide!

Love

Romance

Friendship

Beauty

Faithfulness

Spring of Love

Love . . . an eternal spring
Even if in the winter of an aged heart
It happens to live!

Preposterous

What?
Preposterous, you said?
No, my dear friend!
It is not preposterous to live and die for love,
But to live and never be able to love, certainly is!

Till Morning Comes

The sun has set.
The day wears her evening gown.
The flickering stars are dancing in the sky.
Night's mesmerizing song resonates,
And our hearts, attentively, listen to every note
That nature's harp produces while our lips join in
The sacred silence to worship love till morning comes!

No, My Darling . . .

No, my darling,
Death unable will be us to separate,
For our souls have been interwoven
By the hands of fate!

Her Smile

Her smile thawed mistrust.
Her looks opened his heart wide.
Blooming are love's fields!

Her Name to Chant

Come life, come,
Lend me a few more precious breaths,
For her name I wish to chant once more
Before I die!

A Blessing or a Curse?

Being special to someone . . .
A blessing or a curse may it be.
So, make certain in each step you take
That you both agree!

Happiness, Unhappiness

Oh, you Happiness,
Do not look at me with contempt!
For, I am Unhappiness, your twin sister,
Without whose presence, your name
Unknown through the ages
Would have stayed!

Divine Eros

Oh, divine Eros,
Son of Venus,
Conqueror of hearts and minds,
Better it is for me your loyal subject to become
In your blissful dominion of love
Than to take arms against your sweet tyranny
So that my freedom I may retain!

Eternal Poetry

Eternal Poetry,
The immortal language of the Divine,
The soul of my soul, the breath of my breath,
The heart of my heart, the mind of my mind,
Let me be close to your enchanting bosom forever,
Not even for a moment able am I to live
Without your inspiring EMBRACE!

The Richest of Men

Your smiles . . . pearls
   Your caresses . . . gold
      Your kisses . . . diamonds
         Your love . . . a mythical treasure!

Having you by my side, my darling,
No richer man than myself
Could ever be found!

Wedding Anniversary

A shrine for each year we have been together
I would build up for our love to glorify!

Betrayal

No, my love,
It is not the pain caused by the dagger which
Pierced my heart that makes me suffer,
But the fact that it was your beloved hand, which
Drove the cold steel blade deep into the core
Of my affection, killing thus our love!

Embraced by Loneliness

He was embraced by depressing loneliness
While dancing with the shadows of despair,
But hoping was he, her smile to shine again
For the path to happiness, him to prepare!

Trust and Friendship

Trust's
First step
To friendship
Eliminates
Doubt!

The River of Love

The river
That fed the sea of their love has run dry,
And now their thirsty-for affection-hearts
Pray to Eros
For the rain of warm-heartedness to come!

Mirage

My heart,
Believing in the reality of your love
Made me follow you into passions' burning desert
In search of the promised oasis of our dreams
Where happiness, you said, could easily blossom,
BUT a mirage your love turned out to be.
Thus, under the sizzling sun of disillusion I was left,
Taking sacred oaths not to listen anymore
To heart's fraudulent promises!

Heavenly Love

She asked for nothing.
He offered her everything.
Love made in heaven!

If Only I Could . . .

If only I could empty your veins
From your indifferent blood that runs through,
And replace it with mine,
Only then would you be able
To feel the intensity of my love,
Which as boiling lava makes my heart beat
Ecstatically for you!

Knowledge

Ignorance

Truth

Opinion

Justice

Politics

Time

The Light of Truth

Painful it is for the eyes of ignorance
To withstand truth's light!

The Circle of Life

God,
Logos,
Creation,
Heavenly breath . . .
That's the way life sprang from infinity,
Overflowing thus the river of souls
Which were carried
To the sea
Of being
To
Live once
And return
Afterwards to
The awaiting celestial home of bliss!

Love's Womb

Out of love's womb,
The universe sprang . . .
An eternal miracle of becoming!

Cosmic Wisdom

Wisdom . . .
The conception of the harmonious agreement
Achieved by God between the opposite universal forces
So as to incorporate His divine will into creation!

Destiny and My Path of Life

Once, Destiny and I
Got in the act of retracing the path of my life.
Noticing how difficult my path was, I strongly protested.
So, my angry voice I raised, asking her aloud:
"Why are you doing this to me, when you see there are easier ways that my life could pass through,
without much suffering and pain?"
Calmly, Destiny turned toward me
And explained patiently:
"The path against which you so intensely are protesting,
the one that has been designed especially for you, is there to prepare you to be successful with the mission your soul has been entrusted. Otherwise, you will not be able to help the divine plan to come to its completion,
the way our Lord with necessity
has planned since the moment of creation!"

Reason and Heart

Reason and heart . . .
A conflict has started since their birth.
Reason sees the world as it is
While heart sees it as it wishes the world to be.
No matter what arguments reason brings forth,
The heart turns them down.
Till the moment . . .
A new element enters the scene:
FAITH!

Free Will: Illusion or Reality?

Are we really free?
Free to choose to
Go wherever we please,
Do whatever we desire,
Be with whom we wish,
Pick whichever thing we fancy,
Without coercion,
Without ever being obliged by an unseen force in
A predetermined or predestined way?

How?

How can we have free will to be
Wherever we wish to be,
When bound to Earth we are
With the heavy chains of gravity,
Obliged, incessantly to follow our planet
As it moves around its circumference,
Around the sun,
Around the galaxy,
Around the universe,
Having no chance ever to escape its
Deterministic laws?

Are we free?

Have we got a free will?
If yes, when did it start?
The day we were born or later on?
For, on the day we were born
We knew nothing of
What we were,
Who we were,

What we wanted,
What we needed,
What we desired . . .

Subject were we to our bodily organs
And their functions.
No control had we over
Our heart,
Our liver,
Our kidneys,
Our spleen,
Our blood circulation,
Our brain,
And had no idea
Of how to defend ourselves
Against diseases,
How to produce blood,
How to digest . . .

We had not any control then,
And we have no more control now as adults.

How then are we free?

In what respect?

Is it because we choose A over B?
To be here or there?
To do this or that?

What if our choices are just
The result of the working of nature in us,
The outcome of ideas and tendencies,
Implanted in our mind and soul
By Man or Mother Nature?

In that case,
Isn't our acceptance of free will like declaring that
The earth goes around the sun
Because of its free will?
A stone falls as a result of the same reason?
A seed spouts because of its free will
And that the salmon, after venturing for years in
The ocean, returns to the river where it came to life
To lay its eggs out of free will?

Or is free will the result of our Lord, the creator
And creator of the universe, as they say?

In this case, free will is a gift of God to men
To show His love to us, to make us partners of His creation
By giving us the chance to become responsible beings
That would safeguard nature, obeying God's holy laws
Of the harmonious cooperation and coexistence
Of all living things.

If that is true, then we may ask:
Would the wisdom of our Lord entrust His creation to us,
To our free will to do as we please?

If the answer is yes, then we have to ask ourselves:
Are we happy with the results of our free actions upon
The world God has created?

Are we pleased with the demolition of harmony?
The annihilation of various species of animals?
The devastation of the environment?
The killings and the wars?

Whatever the answer may be,

The mystery will linger . . .
For, we know nothing for certain,
Since we do not know the truth.

Hence,
The only thing we can do is
To believe the one theory or the other!

Faith's Harbor

Over many seas of opinions sailed
The elusive truth, searching to find . . .
Many decades passed without success.
So, to faith's harbor is anchored his mind!

Yearning for Truth

My unsated soul
Yearns to know your truth, my Lord.
Unfulfilled desire!

Truthfulness

Loath
falsehood
to be able
truthfulness to
love!

Democracy

Oh Democracy*,
You most desirable bride among political systems,
Many suitors you have had throughout history!
In every part of the world, you were the one
They were after, but you declined
Their proposals despite the fact
That all suitors tried to charm you with great honors
And by putting your name next to theirs to allure you to
Sanctify their biased politics.
Thus, the oligarchs,
The despots,
The tyrants,
The dictators
The totalitarians and many more,
All have declared themselves your fervent admirers,
Your ardent devotees to you and to your eternal principles
By wrapping themselves in your heavenly gown,
Calling themselves your beloved ones,
But you, unyielding remained,
For you knew that no one has succeeded to measure up
To the ideals your wise father, Solon, has set,
And to the glorious values with which he nurtured you,
Those superb principles
Of virtue,
Of justice,
Of ethics,
Of freedom,
Of equality,
Of autonomy,
Of self-knowledge,
Of responsibility,
Of lack of self-interest
And of the paramount devotion
To the common good and the happiness

Of the people you serve!

It is for that reason, you, oh Democracy,
Seldom have you shown any favoritism
To any of your suitors, for all fell short
Of your lofty aspirations.
Thus, you were, unfortunately,
For very lengthy periods of time
Mistreated, neglected, subjugated and
Exploited by your pretenders:
The immoral,
The unjust,
The dishonorable,
The Ignorant,
The power-thirsty,
The war mongers,
The money-seekers,
Who chose to ignore all that you stood for
And disregarded the common good and
The happiness of the people they were
Supposed to serve. For, they promoted
Their own interest and those of their
Cronies, thus ruining the chances of
Any true democratic society to be established.
For that reason, oh Democracy, I understand you now
And why a spinster, you have chosen to remain!

*Democracy is the combination of two words in Greek: "Demos" and "Cratos". "Demos" means the People, and "Cratos" means Power. So, Democracy means "Power to the People".

Voting and Democracy

Deadlier than bullets have ballots become.
If only the interests of the few they would serve!

Courting Old Age

Oh, graceless old age!
Your unattractive face, many despise,
But your company they desperately seek.
For, how else could the magic of life be enjoyed
If they were not among those you pick?

Editing . . .

Another day starts,
Another day of my life's editing I have to begin . . .

New things to write,
Other things to correct and
Some old things to erase!

Yesterday,
The same things I did
I thought that I had finished with editing
But new events proved me wrong,
Thus, made me start all over again my:

Writing,
Correcting,
Erasing . . .

Tomorrow,
Another day will be born.
The same procedure I will follow.

You see, my dear friends,
Life is full of lessons:
Some good,
Some bad,
Some painful,
Some pleasant,
But life is never boring,
For it is always in motion,
Always in constant change,
And I myself, have no choice but to follow.

So, as life dictates its terms, I obey
Thus, I keep editing my life in perpetuity.
For, an unexamined life, is impossible to lead
To happiness!

The Foe

Lie:
The foe
Of every
God-inspiring
Truth!

Beyond this Valley

Beyond this valley of the here-and-now
Over the snow-covered mountains of life's restrictions,
Lies a world of unimaginable beauty
Of green pastures that stretch into eternity,
Waiting to welcome the souls of the just
To let them roam free in God's domain!

A Poet's Heart

The wind
The cloud
The rain

The rivers
The lakes
The seas

The trees
The bushes
The flowers

The birds
The bees
The butterflies

All . . .

Have a story to tell,
An experience to relate,
A purpose to describe,
Using
A mystic language,
A cosmic vocabulary
Of the origin, the divine
That mere mortals are incapable to comprehend,
Unless the heart of a poet – with the passing of time –
Comes to possess!

Oxymora

Although
We are uninterruptedly reminded of death,
We are all surprised when it comes!
We abhor old age, yet we seem to do
Everything we can to be old!
We have been taught that love is
The salvation of humanity, but we succumb
To hate's demands!
We have seen the horrors of wars, but we never stop
Discovering more powerful weapons of destruction!
We know by polluting the planet we endanger
Our existence, yet we keep polluting it!
History teaches us that things do not change by themselves,
But we keep hoping things to get better
Without us altering our ways!
We have been convinced of our mortality,
Yet we don't make any serious effort
To prepare for immortality!
We are aware of our limited knowledge,
But we never stop criticizing God's wisdom!

Knowing Oneself

Each one of us is three things:
What he thinks he is,
What others think he is,
And what he really is.

What one thinks he is, certainly he is not!
For, he doesn't have knowledge of his real self.

What others think that he is, by all means he is not!
For, others suffer from double ignorance . . .
They ignore who they are in the first place,
A fact which renders it impossible to know others.
Therefore, one's self is unknown to both
In different degrees.
It is known only to God!
Thus, to know oneself
One has to know God,
But to know God, one has to know himself!
Confused?
Join the club!
I am here waiting for a fellow ignorant!

Demetrios Trifiatis

An Infinite Ocean

An infinite ocean
Of inspiration Thou Word, my Lord,
And I, alas, a finite being
Who after so many decades of endless efforts
Has just managed to sip only a few droplets
Of Thy divine wisdom!

The Laughs of Youth

Laughs
Of youth
Turn into
Old age's bitter
Tears!

Good and Evil

The amount of good and evil,
A constant remains
Throughout space and time.
There is no more suffering than good fortune,
No more good fortune than suffering
In the universe and in the human soul.
This is the law of being,
A constant flux of the two forces,
An expression of a single reality in perfect balance.

The one cannot exist without the other.
Even if we like it or not,
Even if we wish it or not,
We have to accept it and live in peace
Or deny it and live in suffering.
That is the will of the universe . . .
A harmonious unity of the two opponents
Based on collaboration and coexistence
Of each individual part for the whole
To be maintained under the watchful eye
Of universal justice!

Man's Character

On the anvil of destiny
Man has to forge his character
With the hammer of experience
And learning!

Like Starving Lions

Like a pride of starving lions,
Lust's unbridled appetites fell upon
The herd of tamed virtues
Devouring them to the last,
Leaving behind only the carcasses
Of lofty ideals for evil's scavengers to feast!

The Sparkle of Wisdom

Wonder is the sparkle
that sets a soul in search of wisdom
aflame!

Death, My Pal

Death,
An old friend, as old as life,
We met soon after my birth.
He liked to play games with me.
"Be ready," he said, "I am coming for you."
I waited, was all ready to go,
No fear, no regrets, no agony.

Typhus was a serious matter back then.
I was a child of four.
In the last minute, he changed his mind
And let me be.

He returned later on though.
Impressive he was, scary.
I was a youth then, and
Knew I had a lot to lose.
My entire life was before me,
But what could I do?
He is the boss.

I fought back, after the accident.
He seemed to like my fighting.
He played cat and mouse for a while,
But in the end, he let me go with a warning:
 "Next time will be your last."
I nodded. He smiled.

Years passed.
I neither saw nor heard of him for all that time.

Ready was I to welcome my daughter.
Anxiously, I was awaiting the marvelous moment.
Suddenly, he knocked on the door.

"Here I am again!" He shouted.
"You have chosen the worst of times", I told him.
"Any time is a good time for me!" He retorted.
"Wait for her to be born, at least," I begged him.
"Ok, you have nine months."
"Thank you, you are so generous."

Finally, he let me off the hook again,
Why? I do not know!

Probably, the cancer was not that aggressive.
Probably, because he knows I am his.
So, he likes to play, to scare people
As it gives him prestige and status.

Since my daughter's birth,
I had some more skirmishes with death:
Melanoma, Apnea, cancerous cells,
But each time, he let me go.

Now, I do not care.
I am not afraid of him anymore.
We have become buddies. We jock and we laugh.
He plays the terrible master, I play the intrepid servant.

You see, my mortal friends,
We must keep up the appearances.
This is the game of life and death,
A game that no matter who loses,
Life is always the winner.
For even after we die, we live.

Cheer up!

There he comes again,
Smiling and cheerful he is, as never before:

"Hi pal, you look great!"
"So do you," I reply.

We embrace each other,
For that is what pals do!
"It is such a fun to have old friends like you!" I muse.
"Let's have a beer before going." He suggests.
"Why not?" I reply, "I am in no hurry!"
He laughs and so do I.
What a great guy! What a PAL!
I could even give my soul to HIM . . .

Performance over.
Curtains down.
"See you later!"
"I am certain about it . . ."

The same game I will play
With my pal once more.
I would even write
A poem about it,
But under a different name.
I will keep you posted . . .

In the meantime,
Enjoy life,
Here and in the
Hereafter!

This is a biographical poem. All health details are true. I am not afraid of dying, but I do not look forward to it either! Not yet anyway . . .

Beastly Appetites

Suffering from his excessive beasty appetites in life,
A man in desperation, turned toward them and asked:

"Why you, insatiable appetites, don't ease your
excruciating demands for a moment so my soul,
at last, peace to find?"

Surprised by the question, his beastly appetites angrily
Replied:

"Why are you complaining silly man,
when you know very well that it was you
who have nurtured us into maturity
by satisfying our every single desire?"

The Stranger

The Stranger: "Who are you?"
Poet: "I am a poet!"
S.: "Where do you get your ideas from?"
P.: "From the Muse, of course."
S.: "Is Muse a friend of yours?"
P.: "I think she is since she has never stopped inspiring me."
S.: "Very well! Tell me one more thing, please!"
P.: "Gladly!"
S.: "Does Muse consider you a friend of hers?"
P.: "She must, otherwise she wouldn't be around me for that long."
S.: "Do friends betray friends?"
P.: "Certainly not!"
S.: "Then, if we see someone writing things of hate, would we consider him a friend or a foe?"
P.: "A foe for sure!"
S.: "In that case, does this person have the right to call himself a poet?"
P.: "No, how could he?"
S.: "Why not?"
P.: "Because he promotes strife and not harmony, and beauty that poetry represents!"
S.: "Excellent, my friend! Now I will leave you in peace."
Poet: "You have not even told me your name."
The Stranger: "I am the Muse!"

Knowledge and Wisdom

Knowledge: The incomplete result of Man's efforts
To unravel the secrets of the cosmos.
Wisdom: The well-kept secret of the functioning
Of the universe possessed by God alone!

The Deception Queen

False crown, with pride she wears.
On vanity's throne she sits.
Hypocrisy reigns!

Unsolved Mystery

Bewildering life.
Cosmos' unsolved mystery.
God's Revelation!

The Poet and His Muse

Once upon a time,
A frustrated poet
Who had not written for a while,
Turned toward the heavens,
And at the top of his voice, he cried:
"Why oh you, divine Muse, have forsaken me,
and now, able I am not, to write even a single line?"

Calmly, the Muse looked at him with compassion,
And thus replied:
"Dear child of mine, I would like you to recall the days
when my inspiration used to flow freely into your heart,
like a river of feelings and emotions which you so artfully
were putting on paper, creating thus poetry of great beauty
that was by all admired."

"Lately though", she continued,
"You do not come to me for inspiration anymore,
as you did in those days. You come demanding from me
to offer you something that you have never been denied:
my affection! But you do it without any humility."

Then she added:
"Instead, you come with arrogance
trying to put words in my mouth,
ordering me to arrange them in the way that pleases you
and not in the way poetry itself would like to arrange.
Therefore, my advice to you, who supposed to be the voice
of my inspiration, must understand that I made you mute
out of love and respect for poetry and not for any other
reason, till you humble yourself enough before this
marvelous gift that God has offered you and me, which is
the language that in heavens it is spoken, the language that
to you mere mortals as POETRY it is known!"

In Search of Wisdom's Trail

Among, the towering mountains
Of menacing fanaticism, and in the midst
Of the shadows of constant fear,
Agonizing humanity, desperately, is crawling
In search of the trail of understanding,
Praying that it would lead it onto the valley
Of God-loving peace where the peoples of the world,
Respecting the beliefs of others in harmony would live,
Glorifying God's wisdom which saved them
From falling into the ravines of voracious hate
Where Man's annihilation lurks!

Lord's Word

Since the dawn of his life,
He was fighting the ills of this world
With the enthusiastic sword of his youth,
Innumerable battles he gave.
Some he won, many he lost but kept fighting
Till his sword was broken!

It was then his pen of poetry he lifted to oppose
The increasing-in number-enemies of God,
Thus, he yielded not an inch to evil's demands.
For, the Word of his Lord
He was never ready to betray!

No Greater Injustice

No greater injustice than this:

To condemn people to death
Just for tender acts of love,
While rewarding others
For committing barbarous acts in war!*

*Brunei is introducing new laws that make sex between men an offense punishable by stoning to death. Other countries that have similar laws are: Iran, Saudi Arabia, Yemen, Sudan, Mauritania, parts of Nigeria and Somalia according to BBC. There are currently 70 countries that criminalize same sex relations says ILGA.

Author's Quotes

Disembodied Dreams

Dreams: Disembodied entities in need of being incarnated into concrete reality!

Embracing Life

One should not expect life rewarding to be, unless its immensity one fully embraces!

Life's Principle

Life: The animating eternal principle incarnated within the perimeter of the temporal!

To Live is to Love

The true meaning of life is only to be found in our serving divinity's will: TO LOVE!

Approaching God

The more we open our hearts to God, the more the barriers that divide us vanish!

Life is . . .

Life is the reflection of the ideal and the eternal upon the real and the temporal!

Experiencing Life

Life should not be seen as a mystery to be resolved,
but as a heaven-sent experience to be embraced with joy!

In Awe Before God

The part cannot possess qualities greater than the whole,
thus Man, eternally before God ought to stand in awe!

Futility

Futile one's efforts to live in peace with others are, if peace
in his heart is missing!

The Secret to Happiness

The secret to happiness is to be found hidden in the depths
of sorrow!

Dignity

Dignity: The epitome of noble actions taking by the self in
defending the divine within.

Honesty

Honesty: An orphan lost in the streets of apathy, desperately
seeking a foster home of concern to find!

Justice

Justice: A child of royal descent hopelessly toiling rectitude's kingdom to establish!

The Wise

The intelligent one is, when from his own mistakes learns, but when from other's mistakes taught, wisdom he earns.

Misfortunes

The mark of the wise is that he would praise God even in the presence of misfortunes!

Being in Love

Loving: The never-ending effort of a heart to possess the object of its desire!

Hypocrisy

Hypocrisy is the rug under which humanity hides its crimes!

Flowers

Flowers: Transcendental ideals of beauty incarnated on reality's plane!

The Key

Knowledge of oneself is the adept's key that unlocks the mystery of the divine!

Ignorance and Folly

By listening to the words of ignorance, prisoner one becomes of folly!

Beautiful World

By inundating our hearts with beauty, we will never fail the beauty of the world to see!

Our Relationship

Our relationship with God is renewed with each breath we take!

Brave, I Am Not!

Brave, I am not my Lord, but one I become Your Word to defend!

Devoted to Love

A heart devoted to God's love would never give shelter to hate!

Opening One's Heart

For the one who opens his heart to love, salvation his soul gains!

Honors

The highest of honors bestowed by Man pales before God's humblest blessing!

Nature and Man

When one's heart is filled with beauty, the whole nature he sees as God's work of art!

Procrastination

Procrastination is failure's maiden that impends one's efforts to success!

Penniless

As long as profit is the master of one's heart, penniless would love remain!

The Epitome

The epitome of our achievements in life is our input of good in the world!

Success and Failure

As the attainments of others never assure one's own success, so their deafening failures shouldn't hold back one's progress.

Irony

Man, in difficult times to God turns and asks for assistance. In good times though he seems to forget His holy existence.

Racism

Racism is the sharpening stone of ignorance's sword of intolerance!

The Worst Enemy

For eyes that dwell in the darkness of ignorance truth's light is their worst enemy!

In Good's Service

Whoever aspires the good to serve must be willing his wages in tears to receive!

Injustice

Torturous and unholy for the soul are the ways of injustice!

Love's Strength

Neither fear nor despair could ever subdue a heart imbued with God's love!

The Cross

The most difficult is not to carry one's own cross but the cross of others!

Divine Breath

The physical and the metaphysical world . . . the same divine breath inhale!

Indulged . . .

A soul indulged in heaven's delights seldom takes pleasure in earthly joys!

Knowledge

Knowledge: God's cosmic treasure, hidden in the depths of our soul!

Darkness and Light

Darkness always dreads light as much as ignorance finds knowledge appalling!

Love and Peace

The world's misery will not cease unless peace and love are enthroned in our hearts!

Evil Men

The evil men goodness' mask wear
for their true nature to hide,
but the venom dripping from their tongues
soon reveals their name!

Wisdom's Sun

When the sun of divinity's wisdom rises, the stars of Man's knowledge vanish!

Alien to Love

The one who rejoices with the misfortunes of others . . . alien he is to love.

Epilogue

about Demetrios Trifiatis

On April 5, 2019, Demetrios Trifiatis has been officially designated as a candidate for the European Parliament. If elected, he will serve together with "Enosi Kentroon" – the Union of Centrists party of Greece, toward attaining democracy in his country of birth and in Europe.

The birthplace of the author is a small village in Greece. It was there that he was introduced to the light of this world back in August 1944. At that time, his country was occupied by the Nazis and the Fascists. The oppressors left later that year. It was then that a civil war broke out that lasted for five years. When the war was finally over, the country was devastated and, because of their political convictions, the hearts of the people were filled with hatred that lasted for decades.

Demetrios Trifiatis learned his first letters at the primary school of his village, but when he was about to complete his initial schooling calamity stroke. His father died, and four years later, his mother. Having no choice, he was sent to an orphanage for three years. After completing his early education there at the age of sixteen, he started working in the day and attending school in the evening.

Wishing to enter a university but not having the means to support his studies, the author immigrated to Canada, Montreal where he started working and studying at the same time. He completed his undergraduate studies in philosophy at Concordia University, followed by his post-graduate studies, also in philosophy, at the Universitè de Montreal. His thesis is on the philosophy of Heraclitus of Ephesus. He studied English, French and German, and upon the completion of his studies, taught in Canada where he stayed for eighteen years. During those years, he got married, had children and became a Canadian citizen.

Demetrios Trifiatis has written and published short stories, wrote the libretto of a historical oratorio that was presented in Montreal under the auspices of the Greek Ministry of Culture. He created a radio and television program of philosophical content that ran for two years. He has authored *Lessons Life Taught Me*, a voluminous book of poetry on peace and love and co-authored *An Aegean Breeze of Peace*, also a poetry volume on peace and love. In *Whispers of Inspiration*, which is a continuation of his first solo poetry collection, he expresses his agony concerning the future of the present world and makes suggestions of how the ills of this world could be healed.

The author was a member of the Canadian Philosophical Association, and became the secretary General of the Greek International Center of Philosophy and Interdisciplinary Research after his return to Greece. In that capacity, he helped to organize a number of international conferences on philosophy, religion, politics and education in collaboration with professors of The Athens University. He became the Academic Director of various private schools and colleges, and out of moral obligation, ran a total of six times for the Greek and the European Parliament. During that period, he came in contact with many politicians, including prime ministers and presidents as well as religious leaders of different denominations. His experiences in this area are reflected in his poem, "My Odyssey".

Demetrios Trifiatis has been involved with humanitarian organizations, having participated in peace events, including that of Malta in 1989 when President Bush of the United States and the Soviet Secretary Gorbachev had met. He voluntarily visited hospitals, mental institutions as well as prisons regularly under the auspices of the Greek Ministry of Justice, while offering free English language classes at his church. In fact, the author has been working throughout his life toward alleviating the suffering of his fellow humans in any possible way, including consoling the relatives of those who have left this world for a better one. In his efforts in this direction, the writing of this book takes a particularly significant place.

The author has traveled extensively around the world, having visited all continents but one. He has lived in Greece and Canada for prolonged periods of time, and for several months in England, Denmark, China and various other countries. He speaks Greek, English and French, and has studied German, Danish, Italian and Chinese. Presently, he is retired and lives permanently in Greece where he writes poetry and shares it with his friends.

other books

by

Demetrios **T**rifiatis

Lessons Life Taught Me

Demetrios Trifiatis

An Aegean Breeze of Peace

by

Demetrios Trifiatis

and

hülya n. yılmaz

Inner Child Press

Inner Child Press is a Publishing Company Founded and Operated by Writers. Our personal publishing experiences provides us an intimate understanding of the sometimes-daunting challenges Writers, New and Seasoned may face in the Business of Publishing and Marketing their Creative "Written Work".

For more Information:

Inner Child Press

www.innerchildpress.com
intouch@innerchildpress.com

www.ingramcontent.com/pod-product-compliance
Lightning Source LLC
Chambersburg PA
CBHW071722090426
42738CB00009B/1847